# Wedding

## SCRAPBOOK OF MEMORIES™

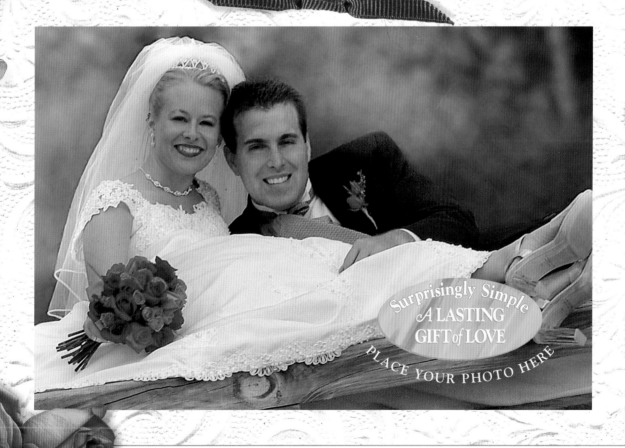

Surprisingly Simple
*A* LASTING
GIFT *of* LOVE

PLACE YOUR PHOTO HERE

INTEGRITY
PUBLISHERS
*Nashville*

# TABLE OF CONTENTS

# How to Create Your SCRAPBOOK OF MEMORIES™

**ACID-FREE PAPER**

*Congratulations!* You have found the perfect way to record and remember your wedding day! Just add memories, and you have a one-of-a-kind keepsake that will be treasured for a lifetime.

As you browse the pages of this scrapbook, think back over delightful memories and unforgettable moments. As you fill each page with your thoughts, prayers, and remembrances, you are creating a customized keepsake that can be enjoyed for years to come.

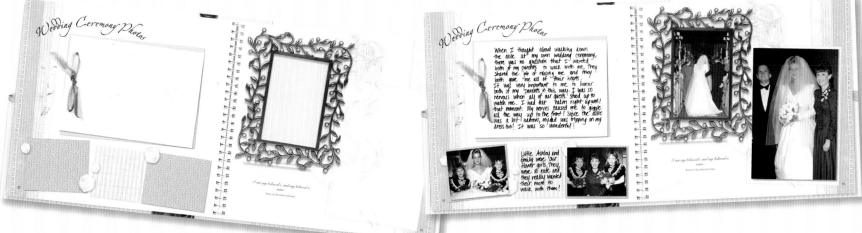

## It's easy!

❶ Record your special memories with the help of the prompts provided on each page.

❷ Gather favorite photographs and place them in the spaces provided.

❸ Tell your husband not to worry—he only has 10 pages to complete!

❹ Remember to tear this page out once the book is finished.

❺ This can be a work in progress. If you have not passed all the milestones in the book, keep the memories and photos and complete them at the appropriate time.

**Scrapbook of Memories™ series**

GRADUATE'S *Scrapbook of Memories*

Grandmother's SCRAPBOOK OF MEMORIES

Mom's SCRAPBOOK OF MEMORIES

Sisters *Scrapbook of Memories*

Friends Scrapbook of Memories

Scrapbook of Memories for my **SON**

Scrapbook of Memories for my Daughter

Christmas Scrapbook of Memories

A letter to my *Bride*

A letter to my *Groom*

*I found the one my heart loves.*

SONG OF SONGS 3:4 NIV

5

# When We Met

When and how we met

_____

_____

_____

_____

_____

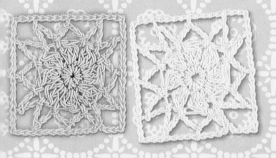

I was attracted to you because

_____

_____

_____

_____

_____

_____

_____

_____

_____

_____

_____

_____

_____

_____

*Groom*

I thank God you are in my life because

_____

_____

_____

_____

_____

_____

_____

_____

_____

_____

_____

_____

_____

_____

_____

_____

_____

_____

_____

_____

_____

_____

I was attracted to you because

_____

_____

_____

_____

_____

_____

_____

_____

_____

_____

_____

_____

_____

*Bride*

*You have stolen my heart*
*with one glance of your eyes.*
SONG OF SONGS 4:9 NIV

# Dating

## Our first official date

_____
_____
_____
_____
_____
_____
_____

## Our most unusual date

_____
_____
_____
_____
_____
_____
_____
_____
_____
_____
_____

## Our funniest date

_____
_____
_____
_____
_____
_____
_____
_____
_____
_____
_____

## Our most romantic date

_____
_____
_____
_____
_____
_____
_____

Our best date

_____

_____

_____

_____

_____

_____

_____

_____

_____

_____

_____

_____

*Delight*
*yourself also in*
*the LORD, And*
*He shall give you the*
*desires of your heart.*

PSALM 37:4 NKJV

# Our Courtship

*God has made everything beautiful for its own time.*

ECCLESIASTES 3:11 NLT

### Our favorite hangouts back then

_____

_____

_____

### What we liked to do together

_____

_____

_____

_____

_____

_____

_____

_____

### Our favorite restaurants

_____

_____

_____

Friends we shared
times with

Things that were especially
important to both of us

# Memorable Moments

The first time we kissed

_____

_____

_____

Our best dating moment

_____

_____

_____

_____

_____

_____

Our song

_____

_____

The first time we danced together

_____

_____

_____

_____

_____

_____

God blessed our relationship by

# Falling in Love

We knew this was love when

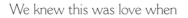

The first time we told each other "I love you"

"Kiss me again and again, for your
love is sweeter than wine."

SONG OF SONGS 1:2 NLT

We fell in love because

God says that love is

Five things I love about you

Bride

Humor
loyalty
Honesty
Romantic
Always surprising me

Groom

# Soul Mates

The goals we share

_____
_____
_____
_____
_____
_____
_____
_____
_____
_____
_____
_____
_____

The values we share

_____
_____
_____
_____
_____
_____
_____

*Love is what binds us all together in perfect harmony.*

COLOSSIANS 3:14 NLT

We complement each other by

_____
_____
_____
_____
_____
_____
_____

We are similar in that

_____
_____
_____
_____
_____
_____
_____

# The Best and Worst

How we support each other

Our best qualities

Bride

Groom

*Love does not count up wrongs
that have been done.*

1 CORINTHIANS 13:5 NCV

## Things we disagree on

_____
_____
_____
_____
_____
_____
_____
_____
_____
_____
_____
_____
_____

## Our silliest fight

_____
_____
_____
_____

## How we settle arguments

_____
_____
_____
_____

# Our Communication

## We like to talk about

_____
_____
_____
_____
_____
_____
_____
_____

## We confide in each other

_____
_____
_____
_____
_____
_____
_____
_____
_____
_____
_____

We pray together for

Our inside jokes

# The Marriage Proposal

*For this reason a man will leave his
father and mother and be united to his
wife, and they will become one flesh.*

GENESIS 2:24 NIV

Length of time we'd been dating

_____

The date of our engagement

_____

Who proposed

_____

Location of proposal

_____

_____

The question:

_____

_____

_____

_____

The
engagement ring

_____

_____

_____

_____

_____

_____

Special details of the marriage proposal

_____

_____

_____

_____

_____

_____

_____

_____

_____

# Faith and Purpose

## Our relationship with God

Bride

Groom

A special Bible verse we like

The meaning of our vows before God

_____

We see God's direction in our lives by

_____

*"But as for me and my house, we will serve the LORD."*

Joshua 24:15 NKJV

# The Family of the Bride

Maternal Grandparents

_____
_____

Paternal Grandparents

_____
_____

*I have you in my heart.*

PHILIPPIANS 1:7 NIV

Mother

_____

Father

_____

Siblings

_____
_____
_____
_____
_____
_____

Nieces and Nephews

_____
_____
_____
_____
_____
_____
_____

Maternal Aunts and Uncles          Paternal Aunts and Uncles

_____          _____
_____          _____
_____          _____
_____          _____

Maternal Cousins                   Paternal Cousins

_____          _____
_____          _____
_____          _____
_____          _____

A heritage of faith

_____
_____
_____
_____
_____
_____

Mother

Father

Maternal Grandparents

Siblings

Paternal Grandparents

Nieces and Nephews

_____
_____
_____
_____
_____
_____
_____

Maternal Aunts and Uncles            Paternal Aunts and Uncles

_____            _____
_____            _____
_____            _____
_____            _____
_____            _____

Maternal Cousins                     Paternal Cousins

_____            _____
_____            _____
_____            _____
_____            _____
_____            _____

A heritage of faith

_____
_____
_____
_____
_____
_____

*I thank my God upon every*
*remembrance of you.*

PHILIPPIANS 1:3 NKJV

29

# Wedding Showers

Host/Hostess

_____

Location

_____

Theme

_____

Guests

| | | |
|---|---|---|
| _____ | _____ | _____ |
| _____ | _____ | _____ |
| _____ | _____ | _____ |
| _____ | _____ | _____ |

Memorable moments

Food served

31

# Wedding Showers

*It was the sound of a
great celebration!*

PSALM 42:4 NLT

Host/Hostess

_____

_____

Location

_____

Theme

_____

Guests

_____

_____

_____

_____

_____

_____

_____

_____

_____

_____

_____

_____

Memorable moments

_____
_____
_____
_____
_____
_____
_____
_____

Food served

_____
_____
_____
_____

# Our Wedding Shower Gifts

When and where we opened our gifts
_____
_____

Gift                                                    From

_____          _____
_____          _____
_____          _____
_____          _____
_____          _____
_____          _____
_____          _____
_____          _____
_____          _____
_____          _____
_____          _____
_____          _____
_____          _____
_____          _____

Gift                                    From

# Wedding Preparations

The wedding coordinator

_____

Decorators

_____

Florist

_____

Invitations

_____

Wedding program

_____

Catering

_____

Wedding Cake

_____

Photographer

_____

Videographer

_____

Music/Musicians

_____

_____

Wedding ceremony
flowers and decorations

_____

_____

_____

_____

The bridal gown and bridal bouquet

_____

_____

_____

_____

Bridesmaids' dresses and flowers

_____

_____

_____

_____

_____

*Through love serve
one another.*

GALATIANS 5:13 NKJV

Gift registries were at

_____

_____

_____

_____

Our wedding rings

_____

_____

# The Rehearsal Dinner

Location

_____

Food Served

_____

_____

_____

_____

_____

Guests

_____  _____  _____

_____  _____  _____

_____  _____  _____

_____  _____  _____

_____  _____  _____

Memorable speeches or toasts

_____
_____
_____
_____
_____
_____
_____

Special moments of the Groom's Dinner/Rehearsal Dinner

_____
_____
_____
_____
_____
_____

Advice we received

_____
_____
_____
_____
_____
_____
_____

*Our mouths were filled with laughter;*
*our tongues with songs of joy.*
PSALM 126:2 NIV

39

# Our Wedding Day

_____ and

_____

were united in Holy Matrimony

On_____
Date

At_____a.m./p.m.

Location_____

Minister(s)_____

*Our Wedding Invitation*

"And the two are united into one."
EPHESIANS 5:31 NLT

# The Bride & Groom

A Handsome Groom

A Beautiful Bride

*And she became his wife,*
*and he loved her.*

GENESIS 24:67 NASB

# Our
## Wedding Party

*Those
who witnessed
our vows*

Flower Girl(s)

_____

_____

_____

The Maid/Matron of Honor

_____

_____

The Best Man

_____

_____

Ring Bearer(s)

_____

_____

_____

Bridesmaids                    Groomsmen

_____    _____

_____    _____

_____    _____

_____    _____

_____    _____

_____    _____

_____    _____

*"A bridegroom's friend
rejoices with him."*

JOHN 3:29 NLT

God has filled our lives with special people

Love
Honor
and
Cherish

"*For where two or three gather together because they are mine, I am there among them.*"

MATTHEW 18:20 NLT

# Our Wedding Assistants

*Those who assisted in
our wedding ceremony:*

Ushers

_____

_____

_____

_____

_____

Servers

_____

_____

_____

Guest Book

_____

*Celebrate these days with feasting and gladness.*

ESTHER 9:22 NLT

49

# Our Wedding Ceremony

Special music, musicians, vocalists

_____

_____

_____

The bride was escorted down the aisle by

_____

_____

Special scriptures and what they mean to us

_____

_____

_____

Special readings and their meanings to us

_____

_____

_____

_____

Our wedding vows

_____
_____
_____
_____
_____
_____
_____
_____
_____
_____
_____
_____
_____
_____
_____
_____
_____
_____
_____
_____
_____

# Wedding Ceremony Photos

*I am my beloved's,
and my beloved is mine.*

SONG OF SOLOMON 6:3 NKJV

# Our Wedding Guests

*"We had to celebrate this happy day."*
LUKE 15:32 NLT

The number of guests
at our wedding ceremony

_____

# Our Wedding Guests

# Our Wedding Guest Photos

*"He will yet fill your mouth with laughter
and your lips with shouts of joy."*

JOB 8:21 NIV

# Our Wedding Memories

*Love...bears all things, believes all things, hopes all things, endures all things.*

1 CORINTHIANS 13:7 NKJV

## Our feelings on our wedding day

*Bride*

*Groom*

The most memorable wedding ceremony moments

_____

_____

_____

_____

_____

_____

_____

_____

_____

_____

Things that didn't go as planned

_____

_____

_____

_____

_____

_____

A special blessing we received on our wedding day

_____

_____

_____

As we left the church

_____

_____

_____

_____

_____

# Our Wedding Photos

*Be joyful always.*
1 Thessalonians 5:16 NIV

# Our Wedding Reception

Location and time

_____

_____

Number of guests
at our reception

_____

*He brings me to the banquet
hall, so everyone can see
how much he loves me.*

SONG OF SONGS 2:4 NLT

Our favorite part of the reception

# Our Wedding Celebration

The wedding reception decorations

_____

_____

_____

The food served

_____

_____

_____

_____

_____

_____

Our wedding cake

_____

_____

The song we danced to

_____

_____

Entertainment

_____

_____

*The LORD has done great things for us, and we are filled with joy.*

PSALM 126:3 NIV

# Our Wedding Reception Photos

Memorable wedding reception moments

_____
_____
_____
_____
_____
_____

_____
_____
_____
_____
_____
_____

*And now abide faith, hope, love, these three; but the greatest of these is love.*

1 CORINTHIANS 13:13 NKJV

# Our Wedding Gifts

When and where we opened our gifts

_____
_____

| Gift | From |
|------|------|
|  |  |

Gift

From

# Our Honeymoon

Where we went

Where we stayed

Activities

*Many waters cannot quench love; neither can rivers drown it.*

Favorite part of Honeymoon
*Groom*

Favorite part of Honeymoon
*Bride*

Honeymoon
Photos

# Newlyweds

The best moments of our first married year

_____
_____
_____
_____
_____
_____
_____
_____
_____
_____
_____
_____
_____
_____

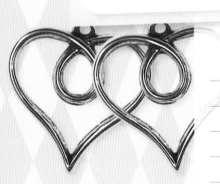

Bride's strengths as a wife

_____
_____
_____
_____
_____

Groom's strengths as a husband

_____
_____
_____
_____
_____
_____

*Live joyfully with the wife whom thou lovest.*

ECCLESIASTES 9:9 KJV

When we're together we enjoy…

_____

_____

_____

_____

_____

_____

_____

_____

_____

## The most difficult aspect of marriage

*Bride*

_____

_____

_____

_____

*Groom*

_____

_____

_____

_____

# As Long As We Both Shall Live

## Prayers for our marriage

*Bride*

_____

_____

_____

_____

_____

_____

_____

_____

_____

_____

*Groom*

_____

_____

_____

_____

_____

## What I prayed for in a mate

*Bride*

_____

_____

_____

*Groom*

_____

_____

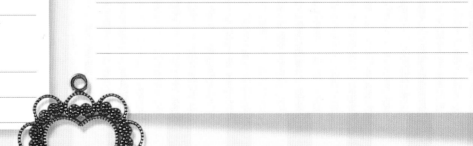

Our dreams for the future

I'll always be here for you because…

# *Wedding*
## SCRAPBOOK OF MEMORIES™

Guide Questions and Editorial Content by
*Amy Koechel Smith*

CONCEPT AND DESIGN BY KOECHEL PETERSON & ASSOCIATES, INC.

Printed in China
04 05 06 07 RRD 9 8 7 6 5 4 3 2 1